EMERGENCY!

SEARCH AND RESCUE TEAMS

SAVING PEOPLE IN DANGER

Edge Books are published by Capstone Press,
1710 Roe Crest Drive, North Mankato, Minnesota 56003
www.mycapstone.com

LIBRARY OF CONGRESS CATALOGING-IN-PUBLICATION DATA
Petersen, Justin.
Search and rescue teams : saving people in danger / by Justin Petersen.
pages cm.—(Edge books. EMERGENCY!)
Audience: Grade 4 to 6.
Includes bibliographical references and index.
ISBN 978-1-4914-8031-1 (library binding)
ISBN 978-1-4914-8418-0 (ebook pdf)
1. Rescue work—Juvenile literature. 2. Search and rescue operations—
Juvenile literature. I. Title.
HV553.P487 2016
363.34′81—dc23   2015034885

EDITORIAL CREDITS
Erin Butler, editor; Nicole Ramsay, designer; Sara Radka, media researcher

PHOTO CREDITS
freetextures: Texture18 cement, 2–32; Newscom.com: DAVID J. PHILLIP/
POOL/EPA, cover, DoD/Sipa USA, 5, David Snyder/ZUMA Press, 7, 9,
Lannis Waters/ZUMA Press, 10, Tracy Barbutes/ZUMA Press, 11, John
Riley/EPA, 13, Roberto E. Rosales/ZUMA Press, 14, Marjorie Kamys Cotera/
Polaris, 14, Michael A. Fiorillo/DoD, 17, U-T San Diego/ZUMA Press, 19, Veri
Sanovri Xinhua News Agency, 21, Chris Corder UPI Photo Service, 22, Gabe
Kirchheimer/Black Star, 23, Ken Steinhardt/ZUMA Press, 24, Marla Brose/
ZUMA Press, 27, US Navy/ZUMA Press, 29

Printed in the United States of America in Mankato, Minnesota.

TABLE OF CONTENTS

SEARCH AND RESCUE IN ACTION

Even though the autumn day is too windy for canoeing, a father and son decide to risk it. When they do not return, a family member calls the police department. Immediately, the search and rescue (SAR) team springs into action.

The team arrives at the river and quickly figures out where the father and son set off from shore. After making an action plan, they break into groups and search all along the river. Suddenly, one group spots the father and son on shore.

In a flash, the rescue team gets to work. They check the boy and his father for any life-threatening injuries. Once the victims have been moved to a safer location, the SAR workers check them more thoroughly to decide if more treatment is required.

Every day, people all over the world end up in situations that require emergency rescue. These situations can involve natural disasters, extreme weather, missing persons, **terrorism**, and others. Search and rescue workers are the brave men and women who put their lives on the line to save these people.

terrorism—acts committed by people who use violence and fear to further their cause

A quick response to natural disasters is essential for finding and helping survivors.

Chapter 1

PREPARATION AND TRAINING

Becoming an SAR worker takes a lot of work and specialized knowledge. Many SAR units are made up of on- or off-duty police officers and firefighters. Some units **recruit** volunteers who have special skills, such as wilderness survival skills or water navigation knowledge.

Certain skills are necessary for every SAR worker, regardless of background. All SAR workers must have medical knowledge, outdoor survival skills, leadership skills, and the ability to stay calm in an emergency. SAR workers must be in good physical shape so that they can handle any situation, whether it is hiking through a rough mountain landscape or carrying an injured victim to safety. They must also be good navigators in order to search for victims. This means that they should be good at using maps and **global positioning systems** (GPS). It is also important for workers to have medical knowledge to provide basic care upon finding victims.

The qualifications to become an SAR worker or volunteer vary from department to department, but most require courses such as the National Outdoor Leadership School's Wilderness First Responder course.

recruit—to ask someone to join a company or organization

global positioning system—an electronic tool used to find the location of a person or object

SAR workers practice navigating by going out into the wilderness.

Often, rescues will involve demanding physical challenges, whether on water, in the air, or on land. Most SAR teams have fitness requirements. New workers must pass a physical exam. Then they must stay in shape while on the team.

While some teams require certain courses and certifications before a person may join the team, other teams provide training themselves. These courses cover skills such as first aid, **cardiopulmonary resuscitation** (CPR), SAR technology, and land navigation. Most teams provide or encourage ongoing training to learn new skills or keep old ones sharp.

Depending on a person's role on the team, he or she may take specialized training courses. These team members may learn about emergency responses to terrorism or how to safely handle hazardous materials. The National Association of Search and Rescue (NASAR) provides many courses for SAR skills. The Federal Emergency Management Association (FEMA) provides Community Emergency Response Training (CERT).

cardiopulmonary resuscitation—a method of restarting a heart that has stopped beating

SAR training often involves learning how to rig ropes for rescue missions.

Personal Protective Equipment

It is important for SAR workers to stay safe while rescuing others. To help with this, they wear or carry personal protective equipment, or PPE.

TYPICAL ITEMS INCLUDE:

- helmet
- safety glasses
- hearing protection
- work gloves
- boots
- water canteens

Since every scenario is different, not every emergency requires the same equipment. SAR workers carry PPE with them to be prepared for any situation. Sometimes they find themselves surprised by the gear they need. It is always safest to be prepared.

Field exercises are a safe way to practice the skills learned in training.

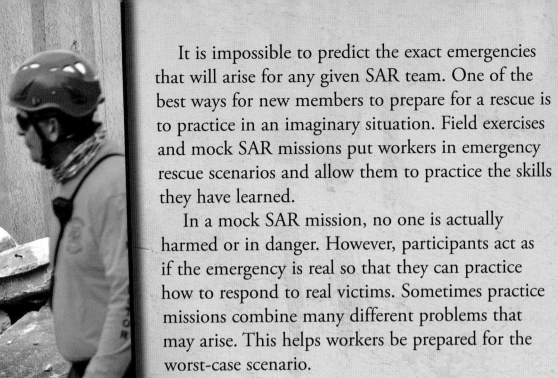

It is impossible to predict the exact emergencies that will arise for any given SAR team. One of the best ways for new members to prepare for a rescue is to practice in an imaginary situation. Field exercises and mock SAR missions put workers in emergency rescue scenarios and allow them to practice the skills they have learned.

In a mock SAR mission, no one is actually harmed or in danger. However, participants act as if the emergency is real so that they can practice how to respond to real victims. Sometimes practice missions combine many different problems that may arise. This helps workers be prepared for the worst-case scenario.

Even seasoned veterans participate in practice missions. It is important for them to keep their skills sharp. Plus, there are always new things to learn from each exercise. By mixing veterans with new recruits, field exercises help SAR teams learn to work together as a unit.

Physical training is very demanding to prepare workers for physically challenging emergencies.

Chapter 2

EMERGENCY RESPONSES

Different emergencies call for different SAR responses. When a **distress call** comes in, officials decide the best approach to begin the mission. The main SAR types are land rescue, air search, and water search.

Land rescue refers to SAR missions that take place on land. These emergencies include missing persons, stranded persons, and natural disasters. Usually, the county sheriff is in charge of coordinating land rescues. Some land rescues require special training, such as high-angle rescue training.

State laws determine when air search and rescues can take place. Some air rescue teams are nonprofit organizations made up of volunteers. Air search may be necessary in missing persons cases or other situations involving large areas of land. Special tracking and navigation skills are required for this type of search.

Like air searches, state and regional laws state when water searches may take place. Like air search, many water search teams are made up of volunteers. Water search may be required to help boaters in danger. Workers on these teams must have strong swimming and boating skills.

distress call—a message reporting an emergency

In 2005 Hurricane Katrina was a natural disaster that required SAR operations. Detailed maps helped rescue workers plan their operations.

SAR Planning Steps

Before an SAR mission can begin, team leaders must develop a plan of action.

STEPS TO BUILD AN SAR PLAN:

1. Collect all facts and information.

2. Determine the condition of the search area.

3. Identify the resources that are available.

4. Identify the top goals and priorities of the mission.

5. Create the plan.

Making a plan brings order to a situation that would otherwise be chaotic. It is important for the people in charge to have good leadership skills. They need to make the plan clear to everyone and answer any questions.

Sometimes local people volunteer for SAR missions that require more manpower—such as large-scale searches.

For large-scale natural disasters, FEMA sets up coordination centers.

RESPONSE TEAMS

Various teams often come together to help with an SAR mission. Different teams bring different areas of expertise to the mission. If the police receive the initial call, they may call in medics, air support, and firefighters. Each group has special skills and equipment. For large missions, a local department may call in FEMA, which specializes in disasters.

In some SAR emergencies, officials may call in volunteers from the community. These volunteers can cover a lot of ground in emergencies such as missing persons. They also have the advantage of knowing the local area well. Officials often give volunteers brief training before sending them out.

Large-scale disasters benefit from a **coordination center**. Workers with good organization skills run these centers. A coordination center gives all workers a known place to report with information and questions. The coordination center often contains a **triage center**, which sorts victims according to their needs for treatment.

coordination center–a central location where workers and volunteers for an SAR mission meet for instruction and supplies

triage center–a place where victims are sorted based on the urgency of their needs

VICTIM EXTRACTION

There are many ways of carrying out the rescues. SAR teams have developed special strategies depending on whether the emergency is a land emergency, a water emergency, or a large-scale disaster.

Some land emergencies are fairly simple once the victim is located. Missing persons, for example, may go with the rescuer and receive medical attention. If a victim is stranded on a mountaintop or stuck in a small, confined place, the rescuer will need to have taken training for the situation and be able to use **extraction** equipment.

In water rescue, there are many rules for safely rescuing victims. These rules aim to protect both the SAR team and the victim. Rescuers try to reach the victim with the least amount of risk possible. Sometimes this means talking the victim through self-rescue. Other times the rescuer may need to throw a flotation device or enter the water to reach the victim.

For larger-scale emergencies, such as collapsed buildings where many people may be hurt, extraction is more difficult. First, the structure must be stabilized to prevent additional collapse. Then rescuers must remove large amounts of rubble to reach victims.

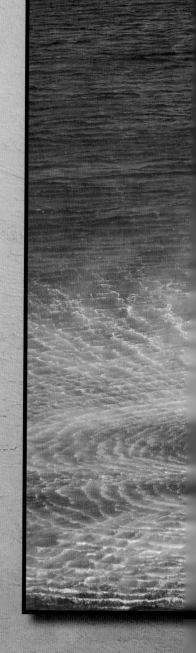

extraction—the act of removing a person who is trapped

Helicopters allow SAR workers to reach rescue areas that would be otherwise difficult to access.

FACT:

SAR technology, such as infrared heat-sensing cameras, can help rescuers locate victims buried under piles of rubble. This technology senses body heat.

Chapter 3

ON THE SCENE

It is early evening when the call comes in. Three climbers failed to return home from their trip to the mountain. They have been declared missing. The local SAR team loses no time in getting to work.

The first step in any SAR mission is creating a plan for the mission as well as a search strategy. The leaders of the SAR team gather all the clues and information they have to figure out where the climbers were last seen. This location is called **point last seen** (PLS). Then they think about the area and consider where the climbers could have gone. This determines the **area of possibility** (AOP). The AOP helps them know where to focus the search.

The next step is to figure out how the search will be carried out. Is the mountain safe to climb? Are there dangerous areas? Will the temperature drop and put searchers at risk? Could the climbers be injured? When everything has been considered, it is time to send out the search team.

point last seen—the location where a missing person was most recently seen

area of possibility—the area where it is likely for a missing person to be found

Mountain rescue combines navigation skills, wilderness survival, and rope skills.

Before a search team leaves, team members must pack safety gear and rescue equipment. They might carry personal equipment with them, while they pack rescue boards and harnesses in their truck for future use. The team makes decisions about which kind of transportation to use for the search itself. The options range from walking to riding snowmobiles to flying helicopters.

Next, the search team begins looking for clues such as footprints or dropped personal belongings. This search strategy is called man tracking. **Man tracking** is a good strategy for the wilderness, since it is unlikely that other people have passed through the area. Clues can make for a path that leads straight to the victims.

If all goes well, a team finds a live victim. Team members check the victim for any immediate issues and give basic first aid. Then they transport the victim to a hospital or other location for more thorough treatment.

Specialized equipment, such as rescue nets, increases the success rates for SAR missions.

man tracking—using the clues left behind by a missing person to locate him or her

Robert Wood Jr.

In October 2011 a boy named Robert Wood Jr. was on a walk with his family in Virginia when he ran off and went missing. His family immediately called for help. Since Robert was autistic and could not speak, the search was especially difficult. He did not follow the behavior patterns commonly followed by missing persons. In fact, he may have seen the whole situation as a game of hide-and-seek. The SAR team set up a plan and followed clues. It was not until days later that a volunteer found Robert in a nearby quarry. He was cold and had scratches and bruises, but recovered quickly.

Rescue workers used canine units to help locate survivors and victims after the September 11, 2001, terrorist attacks.

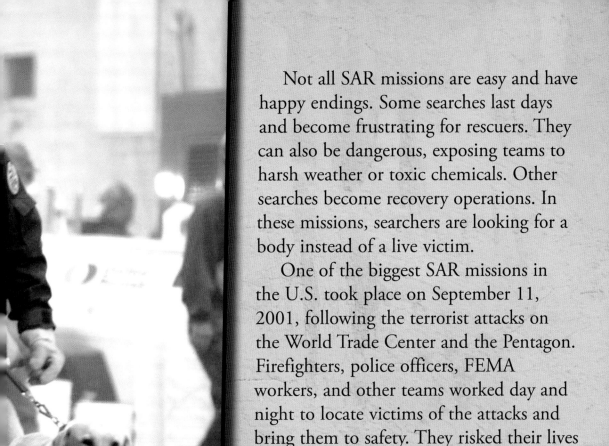

Not all SAR missions are easy and have happy endings. Some searches last days and become frustrating for rescuers. They can also be dangerous, exposing teams to harsh weather or toxic chemicals. Other searches become recovery operations. In these missions, searchers are looking for a body instead of a live victim.

One of the biggest SAR missions in the U.S. took place on September 11, 2001, following the terrorist attacks on the World Trade Center and the Pentagon. Firefighters, police officers, FEMA workers, and other teams worked day and night to locate victims of the attacks and bring them to safety. They risked their lives by entering unstable, collapsing buildings to save the lives of others.

After the September 11, 2001, terrorist attacks, rescue workers wore masks and other equipment to protect themselves from toxic chemicals.

SAR teams make sure to have proper protective equipment for both themselves and victims.

Even when they follow their training and the action plan for a mission, SAR workers can be in danger. Rescuers on September 11 knew they might not survive, since conditions were so dangerous. More than 400 rescue workers gave their lives so that others could reach safety.

In a large-scale disaster, it can be easy for people to panic. SAR teams help to bring order to these tragic situations. With strong central leadership, they give instructions to rescuers and victims alike. They make sure that the rescue effort is organized and that victims get the help they need. Disasters like these make it essential for SAR workers to remain calm under pressure.

FACT:

Ending the search phase of an SAR mission is called suspending the search. This happens when the victim is found or when finding the victim becomes highly unlikely.

Chapter 4

MISSION ACCOMPLISHED

An SAR worker's job is never done. Teams never know when they will receive a call, and emergencies can happen any time, including holidays or in the middle of the night. Teams must be prepared to spring into action at any moment.

Between emergency calls, SAR workers continue training and practicing their skills. They may spend time recovering from the emotional toll of responding to emergencies. Many workers also have full-time jobs in addition to going on SAR missions.

It is essential for teams to have members with advanced skills. Some SAR workers learn helicopter operations so they can search for victims from the air. Others learn special **rope rescue** techniques. Still others learn to predict the behavior of lost persons so that they can set up the best action plan. Each skill becomes another tool in an SAR team's toolbox.

Specialized training, such as K-9 handling, strengthens the entire SAR team.

rope rescue—a technique involving various types of ropes to extract a victim who is trapped

SAR with K-9s

In the summer of 2012, a senior citizen with dementia went missing in Coconino County, Arizona. He had driven a car to a rural area, abandoned it, and then gone walking. When the SAR team was called in, they decided to use K-9s to track down the missing man. Since it was late at night and it was difficult to see, the K-9s could use their sense of smell to track the victim. Before long, one of the dogs followed a human scent and found the man's footprints. However, the SAR workers still could not find him. The next morning, the victim turned up safely in his own home.

Emergencies happen every day, whether they are caused by natural disasters or by the actions of people. SAR teams selflessly put themselves at risk to save lives when these emergencies happen. They give their time, resources, and energy so that others will be safe.

It is not easy to be an SAR worker. These workers must put their skills to work in situations that can be challenging, both physically and emotionally. Whether they are on a local or federal team, or in the police or fire department, rescue workers must be prepared for anything.

Ordinary citizens can do their part by following safety recommendations to stay out of danger. They can also be aware of their surroundings and make sure they can call for help when it is needed. But if they do find themselves in need of rescue, citizens can feel safe knowing that there are brave men and women willing to put their lives on the line.

FACT:
SAR workers can participate in local, regional, and national conferences to learn more about rescue techniques and meet other SAR workers.

Helicopters help SAR teams respond to emergencies quickly.

GLOSSARY

area of possibility (AIR-ee-uh UHV poss-uh-BI-li-tee)—the area where it is likely for a missing person to be found

cardiopulmonary resuscitation (kahr-dee-oh-PUHL-muh-nayr-ee ree-suh-suh-TAY-shuhn)—a method of restarting a heart that has stopped beating

coordination center (koh-or-duh-NAY-shun SEN-tur)—a central location where workers and volunteers for an SAR mission meet for instruction and supplies

distress call (di-STRES CAHL)—a message reporting an emergency

extraction (ek-STRAK-shun)—the act of removing a person who is trapped

global positioning system (GLOH-buhl puh-ZI-shuh-ning SISS-tuhm)—an electronic tool used to find the location of a person or object

man tracking (MAN TRAK-ing)—using the clues left behind by a missing person to locate him or her

point last seen (POINT LAST SEEN)—the location where a missing person was most recently seen

recruit (ri-KROOT)—to ask someone to join a company or organization

rope rescue (ROHP RESS-kyoo)—a technique involving various types of ropes to extract a victim who is trapped

terrorism (TER-ur-i-zuhm)—acts committed by people who use violence and fear to further their cause

triage center (TREE-ahzh SEN-tur)—a place where victims are sorted based on the urgency of their needs

READ MORE

Hand, Carol. *Special Ops: Search and Rescue Operations.* New York: Rosen Young Adult, 2015.

Oxlade, Chris. *Mountain Rescue.* Heroic Jobs. Mankato, Minn.: Heinemann-Raintree, 2012.

Spilsbury, Louise. *Search and Rescue Pilot.* Careers That Count. New York: PowerKids Press, 2015.

Zullo, Allan. *10 True Tales: Heroes of 9/11.* New York: Scholastic Inc., 2015.

CRITICAL THINKING USING THE COMMON CORE

1. What are some types of search and rescue missions? How are they similar to one another? How are they different? (Integration of Knowledge and Ideas)

2. What does a person need to do to become a search and rescue worker? How is this different from preparing to become a firefighter or police officer? (Key Ideas and Details)

3. How do search and rescue workers use skills learned in physical training to help them in rescue missions? (Key Ideas and Details)

INTERNET SITES

FactHound offers a safe, fun way to find Internet sites related to this book. All of the sites on FactHound have been researched by our staff.

Here's all you do:

Visit *www.facthound.com*

Type in this code: 9781491480311

www.FactHound.com®

Super-cool stuff! Check out projects, games and lots more at **www.capstonekids.com**

INDEX